INSTRUMENTAL PLAY-ALONG

Flute

SELECTIONS FROM THE

Harry Potter

COMPLETE FILM SERIES

INSTRUMENTAL SOLOS

ONLINE ACCESS INCLUDED

Professional Recordings

Practice Software

CONTENTS

ARRANGED BY BILL GALLIFORD, ETHAN NEUBURG AND TOD EDMONDSON

© 2012 Alfred Music
All Rights Reserved. Printed in USA.

ISBN-10: 0-7390-8828-9
ISBN-13: 978-0-7390-8828-9

Alfred

HARRY'S WONDROUS WORLD

Music by
JOHN WILLIAMS

Harry's Wondrous World - 3 - 1

6

FAMILY PORTRAIT

Music by
JOHN WILLIAMS

Slowly, with expression (♩ = 80)

cresc. poco a poco

rall.

* An easier 8th-note alternative figure has been provided.

Family Portrait - 2 - 1

HEDWIG'S THEME

Music by
JOHN WILLIAMS

LEAVING HOGWARTS

Music by
JOHN WILLIAMS

DOUBLE TROUBLE

Music by
JOHN WILLIAMS

A WINDOW TO THE PAST

DEMO **12** | PLAY-ALONG **13**

Music by
JOHN WILLIAMS

Slowly and tenderly (♩. = 54)

FAWKES THE PHOENIX

Music by
JOHN WILLIAMS

Fawkes the Phoenix - 2 - 1

*An easier 8th-note alternative figure has been provided.

HARRY IN WINTER

Music by
PATRICK DOYLE

HOGWARTS' HYMN

DEMO 18 | PLAY-ALONG 19

Music by
PATRICK DOYLE

Noble, with expression (♩ = 69)

HOGWARTS' MARCH

DEMO **20** | PLAY-ALONG **21**

Music by
PATRICK DOYLE

Hogwarts' March - 2 - 1

FIREWORKS

DEMO **22** | PLAY-ALONG **23**

Music by
NICHOLAS HOOPER

Fireworks - 2 - 1

WIZARD WHEEZES

Music by
NICHOLAS HOOPER

Wizard Wheezes - 2 - 1

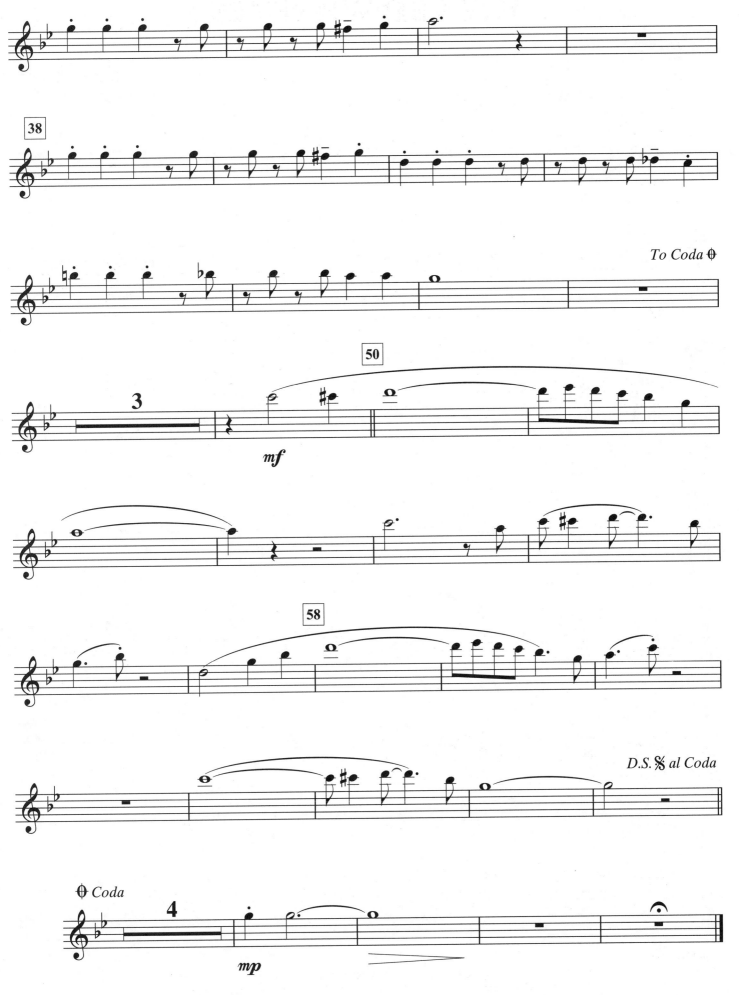

24

FAREWELL TO DOBBY

DEMO 26 | PLAY-ALONG 27

Music by
ALEXANDRE DESPLAT

Moderately slow (♩ = 84)

OBLIVIATE

DEMO 28 | PLAY-ALONG 29

Music by
ALEXANDRE DESPLAT

DEMO **30** | PLAY-ALONG **31**

LILY'S THEME
(Main Theme from *Harry Potter and the Deathly Hallows Part 2*)

Music by
ALEXANDRE DESPLAT

Slowly, with expression (♩ = 72)

STATUES

DEMO 32 | PLAY-ALONG 33

Moderately, with movement (♩ = 132)

Music by
ALEXANDRE DESPLAT

PARTS OF A FLUTE AND FINGERING CHART

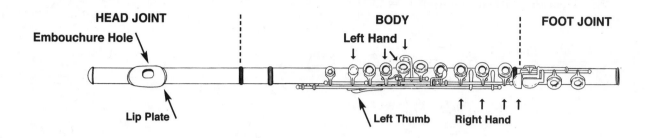

● = press the key.
○ = do not press the key.

When there are two fingerings given for a note, use the first one unless the
alternate fingering is suggested.

When two enharmonic notes are given together (F♯ and G♭ as an example), they sound
the same pitch and are played the same way.

HAVE YOU
SEEN THIS
WIZARD?

AZKABAN PRISON

APPROACH WITH EXTREME CAUTION!